BRISTOL BUSES AND COACHES

HOWARD BERRY

AMBERLEY

First published 2022

Amberley Publishing
The Hill, Stroud
Gloucestershire, GL5 4EP

www.amberley-books.com

Copyright © Howard Berry, 2022

The right of Howard Berry to be identified as
the Author of this work has been asserted in
accordance with the Copyrights, Designs and
Patents Act 1988.

ISBN 978 1 4456 7967 9 (print)
ISBN 978 1 4456 7968 6 (ebook)

British Library Cataloguing in Publication Data.
A catalogue record for this book is available from
the British Library.

Orgination by Amberley Publishing.
Printed in the UK.

Contents

Introduction

Having spent many years living in Bristol, while not classing myself as a honorary Bristolian, I do have a great affinity to the people, the city, and its transport history. To the reader of this, my latest book, the name Bristol will be synonymous with buses and coaches, but over the years the city has also been home to the manufacture of lorries, cars and aeroplanes – indeed, the iconic Concorde was designed and built there. But the history of transport manufacturing in Bristol goes back well before Brian Trubshawe first took to the skies in 1969.

In 1875, the Bristol Tramways Company commenced operation using horse-drawn trams, and in 1895 Bristol became the first city in the UK to introduce electric trams, with motor buses following in 1906, these being operated in conjunction with the tramway. A year later, three charabanc bodies were built and fitted to Thornycroft chassis, before the company took the plunge into full bus production at the tram depot in the east Bristol suburb of Brislington in 1908. To make room, the bus fleet was transferred to the tram depot at Filton in north Bristol. In 1910, the company formed the British & Colonial Aeroplane Company in order to construct aeroplanes, and decided the best place to do this was in the sheds at Filton occupied by the bus department, so the buses were transferred back to Brislington. The result was the tram depot proved too small for the volume of work, and so a new 4-acre site was purchased in Kensington Hill, Brilsington, which became known as the Motor Constructional Works. In May 1914, Bristol supplied its first bus to another operator, Imperial Tramways of Middlesbrough, essentially because the two companies had Sir George White as their chairman.

In 1929 the Great Western Railway bought a controlling interest in the Tramway Company, and this resulted in Bristol Tramways and its manufacturing activities being brought into the Tilling Group, who adopted the diesel engine as the standard power unit, starting many decades of installing Gardner diesel engines into Bristol chassis. Many of the other companies within the Tilling Group turned to Bristol to provide their chassis, and while Bristol continued to build bus bodies, many Bristol chassis were sent to another member of the Tilling Group, Eastern Coach Works (ECW) at Lowestoft, for bodying. The chassis were driven between the two locations by drivers wearing weatherproof suits. In 1943, Bristol Commercial Vehicles (BCV) was created as a subsidiary of Bristol Tramways, and five years later the Transport Act saw the nationalisation of the Tilling Group into the British Transport Commission (BTC). As a result BCV and ECW found themselves restricted to selling their products to other BTC operators. In 1955 BCV became an independent company owned by the BTC and a year later body building ceased at Bristol.

The 1962 Transport Act saw the abolition of the BTC, its road transport subsidiaries coming under control of the newly formed Transport Holding Company (THC). Following a change in Government policy in 1965, the THC started to reduce its 100 per cent holdings in certain companies. This saw the Leyland Motor Corporation acquire a 25 per cent stake in both BCV and ECW, allowing their products to once again be sold to operators on the open market. Leyland gradually increased their shareholding in BCV and ECW and by the start of the 1970s owned 50 per cent, the other 50 per cent being owned by the National Bus Company. In 1975 Leyland and the NBC set up Bus Manufacturers (Holdings) Ltd, with Leyland now boasting a portfolio that included the Leyland Atlantean, Daimler Fleetline and Bristol VR. In an attempt to rationalise the double-deck range, the Titan, a new fully integral 'superdecker' designed to replace all three, was introduced. However, beset by technological and delivery problems, Leyland decided instead to design a separate chassis using some of the Titan's technology, and gave the job of designing this chassis to Bristol. In 1981 the first production Leyland Olympians rolled off the Brislington production line.

Over the years, a wide variety of double- and single-deck bus and coach chassis were built at Brislington, and despite the last traditional 'Bristol' chassis being built in 1982, the factory continued to build the Leyland Olympian. However, 1982 saw the NBC pass its shareholding in BMH to Leyland, who, anxious to cut surplus capacity, decided to close the Bristol factory. In September 1983, the last of over 1,000 Bristol-built Olympian chassis was sent to ECW to receive its body before being delivered to Devon General and registered A686 KDV. The doors at Brislington then closed forever, all work being transferred to other Leyland factories. Despite the Olympian being badged as a Leyland, those built at Brislington were registered as Bristols, with their tax discs defiantly showing them being registered as 'Hackney Bristol'. The Bristol legacy lives on in Brislington; the main road into the industrial estate that now sits on the old factory site is called Tramway Road, and the pub/restaurant at the end of Tramway Road is named 'The Lodekka'.

With Bristol having built so many different chassis types over the years, it would be impossible in a publication of this size to feature them all and still give the marque the respect it deserves, so I have elected to feature those models which I have experience of, either through travelling on in service or from behind the wheel as a driver. As a result, this book covers the MW, F, RE, VR and LH. As with my previous publications I have been greatly assisted in my endeavours by a handful of photographers to whom I am indebted, not only for letting me use their work, but also for having the foresight to record these vehicles in their heyday for others to enjoy so many years later. Each photographer has an initialled credit after their work, and are Alan Snatt (AS), Martyn Hearson (MH), Richard Simons (RS) and Paul Green (PG). Finally, talking of initials, within the photo captions, NBC refers to the National Bus Company, SBG to the Scottish Bus Group, and VCS to London Victoria coach station.

The MW

By the 1950s, British bus and coach manufacturers were moving away from the traditional half cab/front engine design for single-deck vehicles and placing the engine under the floor. This move benefitted operators greatly, not only increasing the available seating area, increasing passenger numbers, but also paving the way for one-person operation by removing the additional cost of employing conductors. Bristol's first underfloor-engined chassis was the LS, which was replaced by the MW in 1957, and over a ten-year build period, just under 2,000, MWs were built at Brislington. The MW (Medium-Weight) had its engine mounted horizontally under the floor between the two axles, and so allowed for the entrance to be fitted ahead of the front axle. All production MWs were fitted with the Gardner HLW engine, either the 5-cylinder (MW5G) or 6-cylinder (MW6G) with manual gearboxes. Apart from fifty-two that were bodied by Walter Alexander for supply to Western SMT, all MWs received ECW bodies, though to varying designs.

The MW was built to the then legal maximum dimensions of 8-feet wide and 30-feet long, yet when the maximum dimensions were relaxed to 36-feet long and 8-feet 2 ½-inches wide in 1961, BCV didn't extend the MW's chassis, but instead introduced the rear-engined RE. During the course of the MW's life, various options were made available including air suspension, this being popular for chassis intended for coach bodywork. Not many operators specified the air system for chassis destined for bus work, however Bristol Omnibus did so on the basis that better suspension caused less stress and damage to the chassis and bodywork and the higher initial purchase price would be repaid by reduced maintenance costs.

The MW originally had its radiator fitted underfloor, part cooled by a constantly running engine driven fan. However, later in its production life it was replaced with a front-mounted radiator and thermostatically controlled electric fan. For improved passenger comfort, an exhaust-boiler was also available. This had a temperature-controlled valve that diverted gasses from the exhaust pipe through a heat exchanger into the engine cooling system, allowing the engine to reach operating temperature much quicker and heat the passenger saloon more quickly.

By the time production ended in 1967, just under 2,000 MWs had been built, a hardy crew of delivery drivers moving the bare chassis by road in all weathers to Lowestoft for bodying at ECW, while those making the long trek to Scotland for bodying by Alexander were transported by rail.

The only non-ECW-bodied MWs were those fitted with Alexander bodies delivered to Scottish Omnibuses fleets. Seen emerging from Carlisle Western bus station in 1970 is Western SMT's DT1395 (LCS 205). It's a sobering thought that the two young ladies standing by the side of the bus will probably be retired by now... (AS)

Would it have been that hard to park them in numerical order? Seen parked in South Wales Transport's Swansea depot are 273/4/5 (XUO 728/9/30), three ex-Southern National MWs. All started life as Royal Blue-liveried coaches but after transfer to SWT in 1971 were downgraded to bus spec. Despite this picture being taken well into the NBC era, 275 still carries the original SWT fleetname. (AS)

The MW5G, with its 5-cylinder Gardner engine was ideal for plodding round the rural flatlands of Eastern England and so was a perfect bus for Lincolnshire Road Car, who operated sixty-five delivered new, as well as several second-hand buses from West Yorkshire. Seen parked in Newark bus station is 2231 (SFU 856), part of the first batch to be delivered. (RS)

A lovely pair of United Bristols (no comments about Dolly Parton's bra please...) stand side by side in Whitby depot. Both are MW5Gs, with 2437 (2597 HN) on the left originally numbered BUE597, while 2539 (539 LHN) on the right, with its triple destination box, was originally BU539. (RS)

Introduced in 1925, Greyhound Motors Bristol to London service was claimed to be the first long-distance scheduled coach service. After takeover by Bristol Tramways in 1936, the Greyhound name was retained for long-distance coach services until 1972, when the NBC required Bristol to adopt the National Travel brand. Seen parked in London VCS in 1970 is Bristol Greyhound's MW6G 2108 (292 HHU), new in 1960. (AS)

The Royal Blue business was founded in 1880 in Bournemouth by Thomas Elliott. At the end of 1934 it was sold to Western National and Southern National, by then controlled by the Tilling Group, resulting in Bristol becoming the preferred chassis manufacturer. Seen in 1971 parked in almost the same location as the photo above is Western National 2269 (68 GUO), a 1961 MW6G. (AS)

The Tilling Group's operations spread across the whole of south-west England, including Wilts & Dorset, which, despite the name, operated mainly in southern Wiltshire and northern Hampshire. In 1964, the company was merged with Bournemouth-based Hants & Dorset, both companies becoming part of the NBC in 1969. In 1972, it was announced that Hants & Dorset would be the name for the entire fleet, but in September of that year 1961 MW6G coach (now relegated to bus duties) 812 (XMR 945) was still wearing Wilts & Dorset's red and cream livery. In the lower picture sister ship 714 (XMR 947) on the left is wearing full coach livery with 1963 MW6G 721 (133 AMW) on the right carrying dual-purpose semi-coach livery. All three are seen in Basingstoke. (AS/RS)

United operated the largest MW fleet with 283 examples delivered new in the ten years between 1957 and 1967. Originally carrying dual-purpose cream and red livery, 435 (2595 HN) was delivered in 1961. As can be seen it was later demoted to bus work but kept its original coach seats. (RS)

A north-east to north-west move saw United Automobile transfer sixteen MWs to Ribble in 1961, including dual-purpose MW6G 270 (2590 HN). It is seen in Carlisle bus station a year later in the company of one of Ribble's standard BET-style Weymann-bodied Leyland Leopards. Maybe both drivers have followed the instruction and gone 'this way for fish & chips'. (AS)

Another vehicle downgraded to a bus, but this time losing its coach-style seats for a set of bus seats, was Lincolnshire's 2076 (RFE 471). New in 1961, it is seen in Newark bus station having just arrived from Retford. (RS)

Delivered new to Tilling's in 1961, 1 BXB was the prototype of ECW's revised coach body for the MW. Three prototypes were built with the oval grille design but 1 BXB was unique in being slightly shorter than the others. It is seen here after having passed to Eastern National before it was downgraded to a bus, work which included replacing the roof panels to eliminate the roof windows, fitting a roof-mounted destination display and fitting a folding entrance door. (AS)

The first production versions of the revised coach body appeared at the end of the 1961 season, so Red & White's UC1062 (110 CWO) from 1962 was an early example. With the introduction of the NBC corporate livery, dual-purpose vehicles were identified by having a white top half and either red or green bottom half depending on the owning company's base livery. It is seen leaving St Margaret's coach station in Cheltenham en route to Blackwood. (RS)

Crosville used a three-letter fleet numbering system to denote vehicle type, chassis and engine type, making SMG453 (1233 FM) a single-deck MW with Gardner engine. New in 1962, it was still looking extremely smart when seen in Caernarfon marketplace ten years later. (AS)

Western National's 1395 (264 KTA) was new to Newquay depot in 1962 but by the time it was caught on camera in Weymouth in 1972 it had been transferred 'up country' to Yeovil. Withdrawn in 1975, it survived as a possible preservation candidate but was sadly scrapped in 2010. (AS)

From west to east, here we see Eastern National's 1431 (MOO 976), one of the 131 MWs delivered new to the Chelmsford-based company. New in 1962, it stayed in Essex until 1978 and is seen on the fuel pumps at Hadleigh depot. (AS)

Hants & Dorset's 1005 (2691 RU) received a rather startling front-end modification when it was downgraded from full coach to dual-purpose status. As well as the rather subtle roof-mounted destination box, it also received jack-knife doors in place of the manually operated coach door to allow one-person operation. New in 1962, it is seen in Salisbury bus station (RS)

With their luxurious light and airy interiors, the coach bodied MWs were the perfect vehicles for undertaking tour work, and Red & White's UC263 (24 FAX) is doing just that. It is seen parked outside Southdown's old Royal Parade depot in Eastbourne in 1968. (AS)

The short rear overhang and positioning of the side mouldings meant that the NBC's National coach livery never sat well on MWs as seen on West Yorkshire Road Car's 1076 (796 CWU), the double arrow almost reaching as far forward as the fleetname. Blackpool is the location, 1974 is the year. (RS)

As well as being the most easterly town in Britain, Lowestoft was also the home of ECW, who built the vast majority of the bodies on Bristols, the chassis being driven from west to east by hardy men whose only protection from the elements was a thick leather coat and a pair of goggles. The roof lights and one-piece door indicate that Eastern Counties LS795 (4821 VF) was new as a coach, although when seen splashing past Lowestoft railway station it had received dual-purpose livery. (RS)

With the driver asleep on the front seat, I'm presuming that Hants & Dorset's 895 (AEL 3B) had popped into Thames Valley's Reading garage to have its missing nearside wiper arm replaced. New in 1964 and fitted with thirty-nine seats, they were downseated to thirty-two to provide additional legroom on holiday tours. (AS)

Newly painted into NBC red and white dual-purpose livery (which included painting over the lovely chrome wings on the front), Midland General 135 (BNN 101C) is seen arriving at Doncaster Racecourse on an excursion. It was new in 1965 as Mansfield District Traction number 213. (RS)

In 1965, Bristol Omnibus took a batch of MW6Gs fitted with bus type bodies complete with folding doors and siding windows but had them fitted out internally to coach specification and allocated to the Greyhound division. In the top picture 2138 (BHU 96C) is seen getting ready to depart Weymouth for the journey back to Bristol. They retained their red interiors when downgraded to local work as shown by BHU 95C, seen here in 1971 shortly after it was renumbered to 2431 and painted into local bus livery. It was then transferred to Bath, from where it was caught departing. Nice Cornish registration on the Morris Minor on the right... (RS)

Knowing how windy it used to get in the old Newark bus station, the chap with the oversized flares was taking a heck of a risk, although his platform soles probably acted as ballast. New to Midland General in 1965, by the time the photograph was taken A295 (DNU 19C) had transferred to Mansfield District. (RS).

That small boy giving Bristol's 2420 (HAE 264D) an admiring glance could have been any one of us, short trousers, long socks and sandals. He probably knew that the grilles either side of the destination display, and lack of sliding windows, indicated that 2420 (HAE 264D) from Bristol's penultimate batch of MWs was fitted with forced air ventilation. New in 1966, it is seen in Cheltenham bus station, and when withdrawn in 1979 was exported to Hong Kong. (RS)

United Counties' last three MWs were the only ones fitted with the updated body style and 260 (GRP 260D) was the first of the three. New in 1966, it is seen departing Southdown's Eastbourne Cavendish Place garage-cum-coach station in 1973. Happily, this lovely coach still survives today in the care of Buckland Coaches of Rendlesham in Suffolk. (AS)

A location where I spent many an hour while on layover, sitting in the smoky canteen eating big breakfasts and drinking good strong tea, was Plymouth's Bretonside bus station, now home to a shopping centre and cinema complex. In happier times, Western National's Royal Blue-liveried 1421 (EDV 503D) waits for its passengers to return while on a day tour. (AS)

National Welsh's U1466 (JAX 114D) stands in Aberdare bus station looking, if I might say, slightly alarmed. New to Red & White in 1967, it probably had good reason to be as it was surrounded by Leyland Nationals, which would see off the last vestiges of pre-NBC variety. (MH)

The buildings on Chester's Northgate Street might be virtually unchanged today but its bus scene is vastly different to that seen here. Not only are the Guy Arabs and Daimler Fleetlines of Chester City Transport no more, neither is the company, having been acquired by First Potteries in 2007 during my tenure as Operations Manager there. Coincidentally, Potteries also acquired Crosville's Chester operations, but back in 1990 when Potteries was management/employee owned. Turning into Princess Street is CMG566 (HFM 566D). (AS)

Staying with Crosville we see G386 (302 PFM and originally CMG386) inside Chester depot waiting its next call to duty. With their centrally mounted underfloor engines and manual gearboxes, MWs made ideal tow buses and several NBC subsidiaries carried out similar conversions. New in 1960, it survives today registered TYJ 424. (RS)

After withdrawal from passenger service, a surprising number of MWs passed to building contractors for staff transport. A Monk & Co. of Warrington operated YBD 202, new in 1961 to United Counties. It is seen parked on the site of Warrington's old fairground on Allen Street and was one of four MWs acquired by Monk in 1973 in connection with the building of the town's Golden Square shopping centre. (RS)

The Lodekka

First manufactured in 1949, the Lodekka was the first production double-deck bus to have no step up from the passenger entrance into the lower deck. This was achieved by lowering the chassis frame, integrating it with the body, and fitting a drop-centre rear axle. The point of the design was to create a low-height double-decker that did not have the uncomfortable and inconvenient upper deck design of conventional lowbridge buses, whereby each long row of seats had to be accessed from a sunken gangway along one side of the upper deck, forcing passengers to have to move into the gangway if one of their 'row-mates' wished to disembark.

The Lodekka had a production life of twenty-one years, and over this time over 5,200 were built, mostly powered by 5- or 6-cylinder Gardner engines, although some were fitted with Bristol or Leyland power units. All were bodied by ECW. This chapter focuses on the rear entrance FL (flat floor, long length) and FS (flat floor, short length), and forward entrance situated behind the front axle FSF (flat floor, short length, forward entrance) and FLF (yep, you guessed it – flat floor, long length, forward entrance) models.

Looking through the photographs that follow, you will notice some differing front-end arrangements around the grille and upper deck front panels. This was down to an engineering option designed to reduce power loss caused by the operation of an engine-powered radiator fan, and to increase the effectiveness of the saloon heating. A gentleman by the name of Wing-Commander T. R. Cave-Browne-Cave (CBC), who was Professor of Engineering at Southampton University, designed a system with two small radiators placed on the outer front corners of the bus between the decks, and the engine coolant was pumped through these instead of the traditional radiator. In cold weather, the air passing through the radiators was regulated by flaps, controlling how much air went into the upper or lower saloon, and in hot weather the flaps could divert all the hot air to the outside of the bus. The movement of the bus was normally enough to cool the engine without needing a fan or radiator in the traditional position in front of the engine, meaning that a traditional grille at the front of the vehicle was not required, but was usually retained. However, some buses fitted with CBC heating had a blanked off front panel instead.

In 1973, a number of NBC subsidiaries were involved in a vehicle exchange with the SBG, the latter sending just over 100 nearly new Bristol VRs south of the border, receiving the same number of FLFs in return. This exchange benefitted both operations greatly, as the NBC was trying to introduce one-person-operation across the board as quickly as possible, and the SBG had struggled to get to grips with rear-engined double-deckers.

The Lodekka was also manufactured by Dennis under licence and was sold as the Dennis Loline. This arrangement was necessary because Bristol was at the time prohibited by law from selling its products to anyone other than similar government-owned undertakings.

Eastern National were one of the first operators to take delivery of the FLF, and over the course of the model's life took nearly 270, including the last chassis built. Their first arrived in 1960 in the shape of FLF6G 80 TVX, which spent all its operational life in Essex. After sale by Eastern National, it passed to Sutton's of Clacton, then Cedric's of Wivenhoe before being exported. It is seen here with Sutton's near their depot on Clacton's Pier Avenue. (MH)

Alder Valley's FLF6G 604 (UJB 203) was also new in 1960 and was the last of only four FLFs to enter service fitted with an electrically operated sliding door. Delivered new to Thames Valley, they were used on services to London for which they were fitted with coach seats, as seen on 604's lower deck. (RS)

As I write this in 2021, lockdown has made popping to The Red Lion for a pint nothing but a distant memory, so the sight of three foaming pints of M&B Light in dimpled pint glasses is certainly whetting my whistle. Red & White's L19.60 (19 AAX) is a 1960 FL6G and is seen in Bargoed in 1969. The FL was the rarest of the 'F' series Lodekkas, with Red & White taking twenty of the forty-five built. (AS)

Seen parked in Camborne is Western National's FLF6B 2034 (414 PTA), the damage to the front dome is courtesy of the low-hanging trees on many of the Cornish lanes, and when I started at Truro depot in 1987, a Bristol LD was kept solely as a tree lopper. You'd struggle to buy a single ticket on many buses for £2.75 today, let alone a week's worth of anywhere travel... (AS)

I know Bristol well, but the location of 1961-built FLF6B 7017 (812 MHW) had me stumped. With no destination to go off, I thought maybe it wasn't in the city at all. Good old 'eagle-eyed' dad spotted that behind the lovely old Austin Metropolitan is Mickleburgh's piano shop, meaning that the bus is coming round St James' Barton roundabout in the Bristol city centre, a view unrecognisable today due to the backdrop being completely filled by an office block. (AS)

Still in Bristol we see a crossover of livery styles, with FLF6B C7059 (504 OHU) painted in NBC green and displaying the NBC double n-sign, but still displaying the Bristol scroll and crest, a practice that lasted well into the NBC corporate livery era. The 'C' prefix to the fleet number denoted an allocation to the city fleet, and C7059 is seen surrounded by sister ships at Lawrence Hill depot. (AS)

New in 1962 and beautifully reflected in Rottingdean Pond as it enters the village from Woodingdean, Brighton, Hove & District's FS6B 45 (XPM 45) is carrying BH&D's red and cream livery. In 1969, BH&D was merged with Southdown, bringing the Lodekka into the Southdown fleet for the first time. Initially, the ex-BH&D buses were painted in Southdown's green and cream livery with the fleetname 'Southdown BH&D' until they eventually received NBC leaf green. FSF6B 2027 (TPN 27) was still sporting Southdown green when seen passing the Royal Pavilion in 1973. (AS)

Crosville's fleet-numbering system indicated vehicle type, chassis and engine, so FLF DFB109 (142 YFM), seen here at Liverpool's Pier Head, equated to a double-deck Bristol F series fitted with a Bristol engine. New in 1962, it was fitted with fifty-five coach seats for use on the company's local express services and as such carried dual-purpose cream and green. The system didn't differentiate between the Lodekka models, hence Gardner-engined FSF 881 VFM having fleet number DFG71. New in 1962, it is seen parked in Wrexham under the floodlights of the town's football club. (AS)

Seen inside United's Durham depot and undergoing some pretty severe mechanical work is FSF6B 289 (8109 HN). It was new in 1962 as DBL9 in the Durham District Services fleet, which was absorbed by United in 1968. Relatively few FSFs were built with the later shallow Lodekka bonnet and grill. (RS)

Looking resplendent in its NBC poppy red is Hants & Dorset's FSF6G 3481 (WNJ 40), new in 1962 to Brighton Hove & District. It is seen passing the unusual Edwardian curved façade of the former Bobby & Co. department store on The Square in Bournemouth, which by the time this 1975 photo was taken had been rebranded as Debenhams. (AS)

Having been brought up seeing not a lot other than the orange and white livery of SELNEC, family holidays to Scotland in the 1970s allowed me to see buses in a myriad of colours. Sporting the azure blue and ivory of Alexander (Midland) is MRD162 (TWG 541), a 1961 FLF6G seen outside Alexander's Perth garage in 1976. (AS)

Glasgow had at that time much to offer the transport enthusiast, especially the area around Buchanan Street bus station and Queen Street railway station. Powering down North Hanover Street away from the former and towards the latter is Central SMT's FS6G B207 (AGM 707B), dating from 1964. Note the top-spec Morris Marina HL, complete with vinyl roof and grille-mounted spotlights. (MH)

Despite being unavailable new to the open market, second-hand Bristols were eagerly snapped up by the independent sector. Standing on the site of Doncaster's old Glasgow Paddocks bus station are former Midland General FLF6G BRB 493B, now owned by Harold Wilson (Premier) of Stainforth, and 822 SHW, one of only three FLF6Ls delivered to Bristol Omnibus but now owned by Dalehill Coaches of Doncaster. (RS)

Another of the Bristol Omnibus SHW batch is FLF6B 7900 (841 SHW), new in 1964 as C7148. In 1976 it was converted to open-top after hitting the low railway bridge on St Luke's Road in Bristol. It joined six other open-top Lodekkas, all liveried to represent the defunct tramway systems across Bristol's operating area, with a name and picture appropriate to the town or city. 7900 received Bristol Tramways blue, a picture of Concorde and the name *Western Challenger* and is seen in Weston-Super-Mare in 1978 taking part in an episode of the TV news programme *Nationwide*. (RS)

Back in the days when VCS was a hive of variety, not only in vehicle types but also in colour, we see Thames Valley's FLF6B D6 (ABL 118B) arriving on the B service from Reading. Nowadays coaches arrive in the former Samuelson's garage across the road from the main coach station, but when this photo was taken in 1968, both arrivals and departures took place in VCS itself. (AS)

Who doesn't like Bristols of all shapes and sizes, and there's certainly some variety here. As well as the main subject, FLF6G 601 (BDL 577B), the first FLF delivered to Southern Vectis, we also see several KSWs, a pair of REs and a solitary LD. The location is Newport bus station with the buses operating shuttles for the 1970 Isle of Wight Festival, widely acknowledged as the largest musical event of its time, with an estimated 600,000 to 700,000 people attending. (AS)

Fresh from a repaint and prior to the application of any adverts is Alexander (Fife) FS6G FRD189 (BXA 454B). New in 1964, it is allocated to Kirkcaldy (hence the K below the fleet number) and is seen on the forecourt of its home depot in 1971. (AS)

Some Tilling Group companies painted vehicles in a 'reverse' predominantly cream with green relief version of the standard livery, usually to signify a higher specification vehicle for use on limited stop or express services. One such vehicle was Western National's FLF6B 2045 (ATA 126B), new in 1964 and seen leaving Camborne in 1972. (AS)

Eastern Scottish acquired Baxter's of Airdrie on 1 December 1962, acquiring a fleet of fifty-two vehicles. As members of the original fleet were withdrawn, they were replaced by buses from the parent fleet, with the transferred buses being painted into Baxter's blue and grey livery. One such bus was FLF6G AA32 (CSG 32C), new in 1965 and seen at Victoria garage in Airdrie in 1976. (AS)

In 1920, Balfour Beatty founded the Midland General Omnibus Company, later merging it with the Notts & Derbys Tramways Company and Mansfield District Traction Company to form the Midland General Group. In 1969, Midland General became part of the NBC, and in 1972 was merged with neighbouring NBC subsidiary Trent. Seen travelling down Sutton Road in Mansfield just days into NBC ownership is FLF6B 613 (528 VRB) – note the illuminated side advertising panels. (AS)

As is the case with the big bus groups of today, vehicle transfers between NBC subsidiaries were commonplace. Seen here are a pair of third-hand Bristol FLF6Gs, parked in Lincolnshire's combined depot/bus station in Scunthorpe. Both were ex-Bristol Omnibus, passing to West Riding as Guy Wulfrunian replacements before making a further move to Lincolnshire in 1978. On the left and still retaining its West Riding poppy red is JAE 630D, new as BOC C7290 in 1966, moving to West Riding in 1969, while EHT 851C was new as C7229 in 1965, moving to West Riding in 1970. (RS)

The Lodekka was instrumental in the success of the fledgling Stagecoach operation, with the first five arriving in 1981, including FLF6G HGM 335E. It came from Central SMT, where it was new in 1967. Altogether, nearly forty Lodekkas were operated, mostly FLFs, as well as a handful of FSs. The bus has ended up in the Stagecoach heritage fleet and is currently preserved in this livery. (RS)

Caught at the Hartcliffe terminus of service 79 is Bristol's FLF6B C7312 (KHW 304E). New in 1967, it was the penultimate Lodekka to be delivered to the company. Ten years later it was selected to receive a repaint to celebrate the Queen's Silver Jubilee and as such took part in a National Bus Company television commercial featuring a silver bus from each subsidiary company. A nice short wheelbase Ford D series tractor unit can be seen in the background. (RS)

The NBC/SBG bus exchange of 1973 saw the SBG divest itself of its unloved new-fangled rear-engined Bristol VRTs in exchange for the same number of Lodekkas from the NBC in what appeared to be a win-win situation for both groups. Eastern Scottish AA966 (KPM 86E) is a 1967 FLF6G that was new to Brighton Hove & District and is seen in Dundas Street bus station in Glasgow in 1976. (AS)

Eastern National purchased several coach seated FLFs with a luggage compartment on the lower deck for use on their network of Essex express services. FLF6G 2610 (AVW 401F) was later subjected to a radical conversion when it became one of eight FLFs converted for driver-only operation. As well as having the bulkhead window removed for fare collection purposes, a small door was fitted halfway down the stairs, behind the driver's right shoulder, to allow the driver to access the saloon. (AS)

One of the furthest distance NBC/SBG exchanges must have been when Eastern Scottish acquired FLF6G AA991G (KDL 145F), seen here in Edinburgh's St Andrew's bus station from Southern Vectis. The last FLF delivered to Southern Vectis, it was exported to Canada in 1992 and after use as a sightseeing bus was damaged beyond repair during the filming of the Samuel L. Jackson film *The Jumper*. (AS)

Moving across to the other side of Scotland we see Western SMT 2425 (ONG 358F), a 1968 FLF6G new to Eastern Counties and seen in Gauze Street, Paisley, in 1976. In the background is JL1887 (XCS 908N), an Alexander-bodied Leyland Leopard that was an ex-London service coach downgraded to local work, sadly written off in a major crash near Kilmarnock in 1977. (AS)

Sweeping majestically from Golden Ball Street onto All Saints Green in Norwich is Eastern Counties FLF6G 442 (GPW 442D). It was sold to Lesney Toys in Rochford for staff transport before moving even further south to Switzerland where it still survives today. You don't see many of those little yellow air compressors being towed around by BT anymore. Come to think of it, you don't see that many Mk 2 Ford Capris either. (MH)

For a fleet that at the time was 100 per cent coach orientated, the purchase by Premier Travel of Cambridge of former Bristol Omnibus FLF6G HHY 185D was quite a departure. Intended as a driver training vehicle, rumour has it that the only person who actually took a PSV test in the bus was the company's Training Officer, who needed to upgrade his licence. The rest of its time with Premier was spent parked in the yard. (RS)

The Lodekka's rugged reliability made it the ideal tool for Top Deck Travel, a company formed in 1973 to provide worldwide overland tours using double-deckers converted to allow passengers to live on board for the duration of their holiday. Seen topping up with supplies in Calais is FLF FLJ 155D, new in 1966 to Hants & Dorset. Thanks to Top Deck, several Lodekkas passed into preservation when withdrawals started in the 1990s including *Deep Purple*, which resides in New Zealand. (RS)

The Bristol RE

Probably one of the most recognisable, and certainly the most successful of the first generation of rear-engined single-deck buses and coaches, the RE (Rear Engine) was in production from 1962 until 1982.

As with all Bristol products built in the 1960s, the RE was initially bodied solely by ECW and only supplied to subsidiaries of the BTC, but when Leyland acquired its 25 per cent shareholding in Bristol, allowing its products to become available on the open market, REs began to appear wearing many different body styles.

The late 1960s were the REs heyday, but in 1972 Leyland, in a joint venture with the NBC, introduced the Leyland National. This was to become the NBC's standard single-decker, and RE sales dropped dramatically. The final new UK examples were registered in 1976, although it did remain in production until 1982, produced exclusively for the Northern Irish state-owned bus companies Ulsterbus and Citybus, and for export to the Christchurch Transport Board in New Zealand.

The RE was most popular as a bus, with nearly 3,000 of the RELL (long 36-foot chassis, low frame) being built followed by the RELH (long chassis, high frame) that was suitable for coach or dual-purpose vehicles, and then the RESL (short 33-foot chassis, low frame). The two least successful variants were the RESH (short chassis, high frame), with just eleven built, and the 12-metre-long REMH, which was designed specifically as a long-distance motorway coach. Only 105 REMHs were built, either bodied by Plaxton for United Automobile Services or fitted with luxurious forty-two-seat Alexander 'M Type' bodies for Scottish Omnibuses and Western SMT. The chassis designation was followed by either 6G or 6L depending on whether a six-cylinder Gardner or Leyland engine was fitted. All told, records show there were 4,629 REs built, of which 3,242 were sold to subsidiaries of the NBC and its predecessors.

Bristol's first ten production REs included the first six numerical chassis, 001 arriving in November 1963 and the remainder in March 1964. Fitted with ECW coach bodies and delivered in Bristol Greyhound livery, by 1972 all had received NBC dual-purpose livery and by 1974 all had been transferred to Western National. Seen in VCS having arrived from its home city is 2122 (868 UAE). (AS)

The MX4 'Derbyshire Express' service linked Alfreton and London and ran via Derby and Northampton. It was jointly operated by Midland General, Trent, United Counties and Yelloway. Seen about to depart London VCS for the journey back to the East Midlands is Midland General's 130 (1384 R), differing from the coach above in having cantilever doors and sliding windows. (AS)

Under the watchful gaze of its conductress, West Yorkshire Road Car's RELL SRG24 (MYG 929D) fitted with ECW's curvaceous early bus body reverses off the stand at Leeds Vicar Lane bus station ready to work the 36 service to Ripon via Harrogate. (AS)

ECW's original bus body for the RE was much more curved than its successor and seen close-up is almost reminiscent of the later style of body fitted to the MW it replaced. Southern Vectis 808 (HDL 23E) was one of four identical RESLs delivered in 1967 and is happily now preserved. It is seen here in 1970 parked outside Ryde Pier railway station/Hoverspeed terminal. (AS)

Only two of the short length, high framed RESHs were fitted with ECW bus bodies: SRB 66/7F, new to Midland General in 1967. Midland General standardised on a forty-three-seat dual-purpose layout for most of its single-deckers and when the RE superseded the MW, they stuck to this specification. They were fitted with coach seats and roof-mounted opening skylights, and subsequently passed to Trent with SRB 66F becoming 145 in that fleet. (RS)

The grandly named Stalybridge, Hyde, Mossley & Dukinfield Joint Transport & Electricity Board was better known to us locals (and probably more gratefully by the company's signwriter) as SHMD. The company had a rather eclectic vehicle buying policy that included the only double-deck Atkinson. In 1967, six RESL6Gs fitted with rather austere looking Northern Counties bodies arrived and 115 (WMA 115E) is seen in Ashton bus station. (AS)

Possibly the most elegant body of all time was the Alexander M Type, all bar one of which were delivered to SBG companies. Designed for use on the overnight Anglo–Scottish services, they were fitted with toilets long before this became the norm, oil-fired heating and only seated forty-two in a 12-metre-long body. Eastern Scottish REMH6G XA274A (LFS 274F) is seen in its original livery in this 1970 shot taken at London VCS. (AS)

The passengers in Hants & Dorset's Duple Commander-bodied RELH6G 1054 (MRU 126F) appear to be looking rather smug as they overtake United Counties ECW-bodied 264 (KRP 264E) in London's Marble Arch in 1976. As can be seen, body style dictated the location of the National fleetname. (AS)

I've often wondered why buses advertise cars – surely every successful sale leads to fewer passengers... Passing the site of the old Wyggeston Hospital Boys School on Applegate in Leicester is Leicester City Transport's ECW-bodied RESL6L 4 (LJF 4F). While today Applegate is a pedestrian zone, the buildings remain and have been superbly renovated. (AS)

When the Severn Bridge opened in September 1966, Bristol Omnibus and Red & White commenced two joint services between Bristol and Cardiff, the 300 stage service and 301 limited stop. Seen arriving in Newport on the latter is Bristol's 1041 (MHW 850F), an ECW-bodied RELL6L new in 1967. Full-length mud flaps were a common feature on coaches but it was unusual to see one fitted to a bus. (AS)

A wonderfully evocative photo of 1970s coaching. C425 (RJB 425F), a Duple Commander III-bodied RELH of Thames Valley, is caught departing a rain-soaked Reading General station on the Rail-air Link to Heathrow Airport, back when the station boasted a petrol station on the forecourt. (AS)

Sandwiched between the front of the old guard in the shape of an ex-North Western AEC Renown and the back end of one of the new Manchester Standards is Greater Manchester PTE 284 (KJA 284F). New to North Western in 1968, the Marshall-bodied RESL is seen pulling away from Stockport's Mersey Square in 1975. (AS)

In 1966, Sunderland commenced a large-scale fleet modernisation, purchasing several batches of rear-engine single-deckers built to the same distinctive and stylish design specifications of Norman Morton, the Corporation's General Manager. They featured sliding rear doors and sloping window pillars with vehicles supplied by several different bodybuilders. Seen after the Sunderland fleet became part of Tyne & Wear PTE is 900 (JBR 900F), a Metro-Cammell-bodied RELL new in 1968. (RS)

Talking of sliding doors, in 1968 Ribble took delivery of ten ECW-bodied RELL6Ls fitted with unusual outward opening sliding doors. Despite being the long RELL they only seated forty-one passengers with single seats on one side forward of the centre door. They were Ribble's first REs and were to remain the only ones with this style of centre door. (RS)

GEM 884N was a unique combination of an RELH chassis fitted with a Plaxton Derwent body. Its registration also hides its actual age, as it was new in 1969 to Doyle of Roundwood in the Republic of Ireland registered ONI 300. In 1975 it returned to the mainland and is seen here in the ownership of Baildon Motors (Dalesman) of Guiseley. (RS)

The low floor height of the RELL/RESL required the rear of the saloon to be raised to allow for engine clearance. Whereas most bodybuilders used a continuous waistrail, East Lancs-bodied REs had a pronounced step towards the rear as seen on Burnley, Colne and Nelson's 92 (LHG 692H). (AS)

Another of those wonderful Alexander 'M' Types is Western Scottish 2208 (NAG 114G), a 1969 REMH6G. Seventy of the 105 REMHs built were fitted with the 'M' Type, deliveries being split between Eastern and Western Scottish. With its chromework gleaming, it is seen parked in Dumfries in 1971. (AS)

Until acquired by Greater Manchester PTE in 1976, Atherton-based Lancashire United could claim to be the UK's largest independent bus operator and between 1967 and 1974 ordered fifty Gardner-engined RESLs fitted with either Plaxton or Alexander bodies. Seen parked in Wigan bus station with Wigan Market as the backdrop is one of the latter. 312 (NTC 129G) was new in 1969 and passed with the rest of the batch to GMPTE, lasting until withdrawal in 1981. (AS)

Apart from the Alexander M Type REMHs, the only other REs operated by an SBG subsidiary were twelve ECW-bodied RELL6Gs delivered to Alexander (Fife) in 1968. Initially based in Kirkcaldy, Fife operated throughout the ancient kingdom of Fife with a network of services spreading as far as Dundee and Edinburgh and express services as far west as Glasgow, this making Fife reputedly the most profitable SBG subsidiary. Seen parked in Dundee Seagate bus station is FE30 (JXA 930F). (AS)

Having only been acquainted with the NBC red of Ribble, a move to Bristol in 1979 saw my introduction to NBC green. Imagine my delight (I'm easily pleased) when I found that our suburb was the only stop betwixt Bristol and Cardiff on the X10 'Cardiff Flyer' service, jointly operated by Bristol and National Welsh. I was able to see both red and green ECW DP-bodied REs in one place at the same time. One of the regular performers from across the water was SAX 6G, seen accelerating off St James Barton roundabout just prior to arriving in Bristol Marlborough Street bus station (AS)

When operating the overnight London–Penzance service back in the late 1980s/early 1990s it was almost like stepping back in time when we called at Taunton in the early hours and saw Southern National's 1468 (RDV 419H) parked up, still carrying NBC dual-purpose livery. New to Western National as a Royal Blue coach in 1970, it remained an active member of the Southern National fleet until 1994, years after all its contemporaries had been withdrawn. (RS)

The lack of destination isn't sloppiness on the part of the driver, but an indication that all is not what it seems. Leicester City Transport's 132 (TRY 132H) is well out of its home territory having been hired by South Yorkshire PTE during a shortage of serviceable buses within its own fleet. Seen in Sheffield, it is an ECW-bodied RELL6L new in 1970. (RS)

The height and number of the steps to get into and out of Aldershot & District's Marshall-bodied RELL6G 604 (UOU 604H) make us realise why bus travel hasn't always been accessible to all. Seen in Basingstoke bus station waiting for its loading bay to become free when brand new in 1970, the Hampshire 'OU' registration identifier would, a couple of years later, transfer to the chassis' home city of Bristol. (AS)

North Western's REs were fitted with an eclectic mix of bodies, with batches of Marshall, ECW (both bus and coach) and, as seen here, Alexander 'Y' Types in the fleet. RELL6G 328 (NJA 328H) was new in 1970 and was part of the North Western fleet that was transferred to SELNEC PTE in 1972. It is seen in its home depot of Charles Street, Stockport. (AS)

I had to do a double take to work out that the girl in the red coat trying to board United's 4219 (DHN 719J) didn't have an extremely long and angular left leg! Seen when new in 1970, the ECW dual-purpose-bodied RELL6G was captured in Carlisle's Lowther Street bus station about to depart on the trunk route to Newcastle. (AS)

As mentioned earlier, despite the introduction of the NBC corporate identity, Bristol Omnibus' city fleet displayed the Bristol scroll. However, C1158 (WAE 791H) is missing its 'official' fleetname. It is caught between the peaks parked at its allocated depot, Lawrence Hill, after having operated a 'short working' on the 88, running only as far as Lawrence Hill. It is fitted with ECW's flat front bus body, complete with forty-four seats and dual doors. (AS)

In 1971, Eastern National received several forty-two-seat Plaxton Panorama Elite-bodied RELHs to undertake their extended tour programme. Fitted with tinted windows, reclining seats and bedecked with additional brightwork and wheel trims, they were quite rightly the pride of the fleet. Whether 9424 (LWC 975J) was actually en route to Switzerland is not known, but it was definitely on Prittlewell Chase in Southend when captured on film. (AS)

North Western's route between Altrincham and Warrington passed under the Bridgewater canal via the 8-foot 9-inch high bridge at Dunham Massey. To do so, buses with specially contoured roofs to match the profile of the bridge were required, the first such being a batch of Strachan's-bodied Bedford VALs. These were replaced in 1971 by nine ECW-bodied RELL6Ls, and showing the distinctive roof is 375 (SJA 375J), seen at Altrincham when new. (AS)

By the time the Plaxton Panorama Elite was in production, sliding windows were an unusual fitment to coaches; however, Red & White specified them on the two RELH6G tour coaches delivered in 1971. When Red & White was absorbed into National Welsh both received conventional windows. The second of the pair, RC172 (XWO 937J), is seen in Monmouth. (AS)

For the 1972 season, ECW introduced a new style of coach body that, apart from a handful of Leyland Leopards for SELNEC, was built exclusively on the RELH chassis, of which all were delivered to the NBC. Seen in London VCS is Crosville's CRL261 (TFM 261K), one of the last coaches delivered in their black and cream livery as the last part of the batch of ten arrived in National white. (AS)

Gelligaer UDC operated its first motor bus service in 1928, and continued to serve the Bargoed area until 1 April 1974, where under local government reorganisation the Gelligaer fleet was merged with those of neighbouring Bedwas & Machen UDC and Caerphilly UDC to form the new Rhymney Valley District Council fleet. Seen in Hengoed depot is Gelligaer's 43 (KTX 243L), a 1973 ECW-bodied RESL6L. In the lower picture we see the same bus but in Rhymney Valley livery. A nice touch by the painter was to colour the Bristol RE badge on the front to match the vehicle's livery. Sadly, the bus was scrapped in 1978 following an accident. (AS/RS)

When plans for deregulation of the bus industry were beginning to surface, East Staffordshire District Council decided that rather than engage in a possible costly bus war, it would merge its bus interests with those of local independent Stevenson's of Uttoxeter, with Stevenson's having the controlling share. This took place on 1 October 1985, and seen just four weeks earlier is East Staffordshire's 1 (YED 274K), a 1972 Bristol RESL6L with East Lancs body that had been purchased from Warrington. (AS)

The Reading–Heathrow Railair link still runs today, although not using ECW coach-bodied REs. Seen outside Reading station is Alder Valley's 67 (KBL 228L), an RELH6G new in 1973. (RS)

Seen in Bridlington is East Yorkshire's 600 (PHN 178L), an ECW-bodied RELL6G with a rather startling body conversion. New as United's 4278, it was converted from a conventional single-decker for use in Scarborough but passed to East Yorkshire when the Scarborough operations of United were transferred to that operator. (RS)

Just take a look at those classics behind Blackburn Transport's 3 (STC 887L). A Mk1 Ford Escort, Austin 1100 and what looks like a Vauxhall Viva, all vying to be first away from the lights. Number 3 was a 1973 Bristol RESL6L with East Lancs body, new to Darwen Corporation, and seen in Darwen marketplace in 1975. (AS)

Devon General's bus operations were transferred to Western National in 1971. However, the Devon General name was retained for services throughout south and east Devon, with vehicles painted NBC poppy red rather than the leaf green of Western National. Showing off its dual-purpose livery to good effect as it travels down The Strand in Torquay is Plaxton Panorama Elite Express-bodied RELH6L 2503 (PUO 503M. (AS)

In 1983, Western National was split into four separate companies in readiness for deregulation, the north Devon operating area becoming North Devon Ltd trading as Red Bus. The sticker on the side of Plaxton Panorama Elite-bodied RELH6L 2504 (GFJ 670N) really does say 'This is now a Red Bus'. It is seen departing Marlborough Street bus station in Bristol on a National Express duplicate to Birmingham, the driver still sporting his NBC issue cap. (RS)

Western National's last RE coaches were five Plaxton Panorama Elite-bodied RELH6Ls delivered in 1974 and included 2418 (RHT 418N), seen on layover in Penzance. When Western National was split in 1983, vehicles based at the Cornish depots received Cornwall Busways branding, National Express-liveried coaches received Cornwall Coachways and coaches on the dedicated Cornwall–Plymouth express services were painted gold and black (the Cornish colours) with Cornwall Express names. (RS)

Fylde Borough waited until almost the last minute to buy its only REs when it took delivery of five ECW-bodied RESL6Ls in 1975. All were fitted with dual-purpose seating and stayed with Fylde until 1993 when they were sold en masse to prolific RE operator Northern Bus of North Anston. The last of the batch was 41 (HRN 108N), seen in Lytham Square when two months old. (AS)

Despite being removed from the mainland sales catalogue in 1976, the RE remained in production for Ulsterbus and Citybus in Northern Ireland until 1983. Most received Alexander (Belfast) bodies such as 82-DL-1420, previously 2451 (WOI 2451) in the Ulsterbus fleet but seen here in the ownership of Lough Swilly. Incorporated in 1853, Lough Swilly was the oldest transport company in the world until they ceased trading in 2014 after 161 years of operation. (PG)

The last RE is something a little bit different. VHK 177L was new in 1972 to Tilling's Transport, passing to Eastern National in 1978. In 1981, its original ECW coach body was rebuilt by ECW as the prototype B51 coach body. As all subsequent B51s were fitted to Leyland Leopards or Tigers, VHK remained unique. In 1985 it passed to Badgerline as their 2079 and was reregistered 929 CVJ. Seen at Blackpool in its original livery with Eastern National, the Badgerline photo shows it arriving at Bristol Marlborough Street bus station. (RJ)

The Bristol VR

The VR (Vertical Rear) was intended as a competitor to the Leyland Atlantean and Daimler Fleetline, with the original design intended for both single-deck or double-deck bodywork. Two prototypes were built in 1966 featuring longitudinally mounted engines sited behind the offside rear wheels and coupled to a Self-Changing Gears semi-automatic gearbox. In order to keep the height of the VR down, a drop-centre rear axle and low frame were used. The chassis was launched at the 1966 Earls Court Motor Show, with two prototypes receiving eighty-seat ECW bodies. They entered service shortly afterwards, one with Central SMT and one with Bristol Omnibus designated VRS (VR Short) and VRL (VR Long).

A year later, Bristol introduced a new version, the VRT, which had a more conventional transverse-engined layout, power units supplied by Gardner and Leyland. By now it had been decided that the VR would only be offered as a double-deck bus but with a choice of two frame heights. The introduction of the VRT was rather timely, as in 1968 the British Government introduced a grant scheme that was intended to modernise bus fleets and speed up the introduction of driver-only operation. The conditions of the grant specified that vehicles should be transverse rear-engined and as a result only thirty VRLs were built for the UK market, all fitted with ECW coach bodies complete with a large luggage area at the rear and delivered to Standerwick for use on long-distance express services.

The first production VRTs entered service with Eastern Scottish, but fairly soon started to experience problems. The mechanical linkage for the throttle cable didn't work as well as planned; poor ventilation around the engine compartment caused overheating and failure of the power unit during intensive operation; and the gearbox output drive (known as the mitre box) caused stress on the bearings. Soon the engineering teams at both Bristol and Leyland were hard at work trying to iron out these issues. It was a combination of these reliability issues, as well as the SBG's dislike of buses that didn't have rugged and basic mechanicals, which led them to enter into the SBG/NBC vehicle exchange previously mentioned in the chapter on the Lodekka.

In 1970, the series 2 VRT was introduced, fitted with power steering as standard, a hydraulic throttle, uprated engine bay complete with fan and extraction system, and improvements to the gearbox drive system. Reliability increased to such an extent that as well as the NBC making the ECW-bodied VRT its standard double-decker, the SBG became a convert and started ordering the VRT in fairly large numbers. Other changes including a replacement of the single-piece wrap-around engine compartment door with a three-piece version with a lift-up rear section and swing out sides. The Series 3 VRT arrived in 1974, with the engine compartment redesigned to meet new noise legislation, and the ventilation grills being moved from alongside the engine to just below the top deck window. By the time the last VRT was built in 1981, just over 4,500 had been built.

As with most Bristol chassis codes, the VRT's was logical, being the letters VRT, followed by the height, length and series, and finishing with engine type.

The chassis types are as follows:

LH – Long/high series 1; LH2 – series 2; LH3 – series 3
LL – Long/low series 1; LL2 – series 2; LL3 – series 3
SL – Short/low series 1; SL2 – series 2; SL3 – series 3

Engines:

6LXB – Gardner 6LXB
501 – Leyland 501
680 – Leyland 0680

Meaning a VRT/SL3/501 would be a short, low, series 3 VRT fitted with a Leyland 501 engine.

The two VR prototypes were recognisable as, having longitudinal engines, they were able to have windows along the whole of the lower deck. After their demonstration days were over, both saw service with Bristol Omnibus before passing to Osbornes of Tollesbury, who had a liking for former demonstration vehicles. VRX/2 HHW933D is seen parked in Tollesbury garage, where both buses reportedly spent quite a lot of their time! (AS)

The series one VRT/LL was only built for Eastern Scottish, twenty-five buses fitted with eighty-two-seat ECW bodies in 1968. AA282 (LFS 282F) is seen in 1971 turning out of Edinburgh's St Andrews Square bus station having suffered some rather nasty nearside skirt damage during its short life. (AS)

Ribble showed great bravery (some may say something else) by choosing the relatively unproven VR chassis for its third generation of double-deck express coaches. The first of the luxurious ECW-bodied VRL/LH coaches, 50 (FCK 450G) is seen in London VCS when nearly new. Delivered in 1968 to Ribble's Standerwick subsidiary, it was nearly two years before the next of the batch arrived. (AS)

Avid FLF users Eastern National were one of the operators involved in the SBG/NBC vehicle exchange mentioned earlier and received VRT/SL6G SMS38H from Alexander (Midland). Still carrying Alexander's blue livery with Eastern National fleetnames applied, passengers used to travelling on Eastern National's luxurious coach seated FLFs must have been disappointed to see such a vehicle turn up for the journey home from London to Essex. (AS)

Another VR involved in the exchange was OCS 594H, new to Western SMT and joined Alder Valley when coming south. In 1981 it was acquired by Top Deck Travel, who converted the lower deck to living accommodation. Seen in Parliament Square, by now Top Deck were concentrating more on European destinations – just as well considering how close to the ground the VRs engine was. (AS)

In its entire existence, Gelligaer only purchased nine new double-deck buses, with the three Northern Counties-bodied VRT/SL2s that arrived in 1971 being the first for over eleven years. They were also the only rear-engine deckers to be purchased before the fleet was absorbed into the Rhymney Valley District Council undertaking. 39 (BTX 539J) is seen at Hengoed depot in 1972. (AS)

Merseyside PTE were the only customer for the long high-framed VRT/LH, taking a batch of fifty-nine with Gardner engines and East Lancs bodies between 1970 and 1971. Sixty chassis were actually built but chassis number 102 was destroyed by fire at the East Lancs factory. One of the later deliveries was 2071 (YKF 709K), seen at Liverpool Pier Head bus station in 1972. (AS)

The VRLs were very imposing vehicles, and 78 (PRN 78K) has certainly caught the eye of the motorcycle policeman as it turns into London VCS. Ribble's management thought the VRLs looked bland in all-over white so painted 78 in this experimental blue relief livery. NBC management had different ideas however, and it was soon repainted back into corporate livery. Stability issues caused by having the engine located vertically, longitudinally and cantilevered out behind the rear wheels, together with several engine fires, meant the VRLs didn't last long in their intended role. As they were unsuitable for downgrading to service work, by 1977 they had all been sold by Ribble to new owners. Margo of Streatham purchased fourteen including OCK 65K for use on London tourist work, and it is seen in its second life painted in Thomas Cook livery rounding Parliament Square in Westminster in 1978. (AS)

Sheffield Corporation purchased eighteen East Lancs-bodied VRT/SL6Gs in 1972, non-standard vehicles in a predominantly Leyland fleet. Transferred to South Yorkshire PTE in 1974, in 1980 they were withdrawn en masse and sold to the NBC, six joining Crosville and twelve going to Maidstone & District. In 1977 SYPTE chose 271 (OWE 271K) to be painted in a silver livery for the Queen's Silver Jubilee and is seen here on Flat Street in Sheffield. 278 (OWE 278K) was one of the twelve that headed south, becoming 5771 in the M & D fleet. (RS top, AS bottom)

Only Bristol Omnibus and Southdown purchased flat front VRs with dual doors (and in fact both were the biggest purchasers of dual-door VRs in general) and in 1982 Bristol acquired ten of Southdown's for use on city services. New as Southdown's 537, ECW-bodied VRT/SL6G WUF 537K became MR5209 in the Bristol fleet and is seen in the city centre en route to Knowle West. (RS)

Only three independent operators purchased new VRs, and Hutchings & Cornelius of South Petherton was the first, with ECW-bodied VRT/SL6G RYA 700L arriving in 1972. Seen leaving Yeovil bus station with stablemate CYA 181J, a Plaxton Derwent-bodied AEC Reliance in the background and fellow South Petherton operator Safeway's Duple Britannia-bodied Reliance TYD 888 to its left, it ended its days with Stevenson of Spath, one of the other two operators to buy a new VR. (RS)

An extremely smart looking ECW-bodied VRT/SL is NUD 109L, new to Oxford-South Midland but seen here with Eagles and Crawford of Mold. It's amazing what a simple sweep of a livery stripe can do in making the bus look more modern than it was, as when the photo was taken the bus was getting on for sixteen years old. (MH)

Reading Transport could always be relied upon to order something diverse, and between 1971 and 1977 purchased fifty of these 'jumbo' Northern Counties-bodied VRT/LLs, the last examples of which weren't withdrawn until 1990. New in 1974, 65 (NRD 65M) is seen in Broad Street, Reading, when just six months old. (AS)

Cardiff City Transport was unusual for a municipal operator in ordering VRs with three different body styles – ECW, Alexander and, as seen here, Willowbrook. I'm not sure why Cardiff decided to call their drivers 'operators' but to some drivers (sorry, operators), meeting people is seen as the biggest single disadvantage of the job! 325 (SWO 325S) was new in 1978 and was caught on camera in Cardiff bus station. (AS)

A leaf green PMT bus when we all know that the Potteries fleet was poppy red? The reason was 614 (REH 814M) had just returned from long-term loan to Crosville when seen outside Stoke garage in 1976. Many years later, the Wirral and Chester part of the Crosville empire would come under Potteries control, but by then all the buses were painted in the same white, pink and purple livery anyway. (AS)

The Daimler Fleetline was West Midland's PTE's standard double-decker but a supply problem in the mid-1970s saw them take 200 VRT/SL6Gs fitted with locally built MCW bodies. They were among the few VRs to feature an engine bustle similar to the Atlantean and Fleetline. Seen with what looks like the Bionic Woman about to dash across its bows is 4696 (JOV 696P). New in 1975, like most of its stablemates it had a relatively short life in the Midlands and was scrapped in 1986. (RS)

I've included this picture of brand new C5051 (LHT 727P) of Bristol Omnibus because it shows the diversity of vehicles that could be found inside Lawrence Hill depot. On the left is recently withdrawn Bristol LS 2844 (PHW 934), in the background is 965 EHW, one of the training fleet's LD Lodekkas, while to the right is a bus I remember from my days in the Bristol Omnibus Preservation Society – dual-door ECW-bodied Bristol L5G C2736 (LHY 976). New in 1949, by the time this picture was taken it had already been in preservation for ten years. (AS)

In order to transport some of the thousand-or-so people who worked at their facility at Harwell near Didcot, the Atomic Energy Research Establishment operated a sizeable fleet of staff buses, all of which were bought new. After purchasing a fleet of eleven AEC Regent Vs in 1962, the next double-deckers bought were seven ECW-bodied VRT/SLs that arrived between 1977 and 1979. Two of the first are seen here in the shape of 112 and 113 (RAN 645/6R), seen at Harwell Visitor Centre in 1979. (AS)

We move from the graceful curves of the ECW body to something the complete opposite. In 1976, Burnley & Pendle took delivery of fourteen East Lancs-bodied VRT/SLs fitted with Gardner 6LXB engines, followed two years later by a further ten. The original fourteen were all withdrawn by 1991, finding new homes with three independent operators – Hogg of Boston and Thomas of Porth taking four each and Hunter of Garston the other six. 164 (URN 164R) was the last of the batch and served Thomas of Porth for a further ten years after withdrawal by Burnley. (AS)

A bit of topless action now. Despite operating a substantial open-top fleet in its own right, in certain locations Guide Friday started working in conjunction with the local bus company whereby the bus company supplied the vehicles and Guide Friday looked after the admin and tour guide. Bath was one such city, and Badgerline's 8621 (LEU 269P) waits time on Terrace Walk. New to Cheltenham District Traction in 1976 as a conventional closed-top bus, after transfer to Bristol Omnibus, it was converted to open top in 1986 and passed to Badgerline in 1990. In the lower picture, Quantock Motor Services' former Hants & Dorset ECW-bodied VR UFX 856S is seen climbing Countesbury Hill out of Lynmouth with the stunning North Devon coast as a backdrop. (RS top, MH bottom)

I stand to be corrected but I believe it was supply problems at ECW in 1977/8 that led the NBC to look for an alternative double-deck bodybuilder, resulting in Northern and East Kent receiving Willowbrook-bodied VRs fitted with ECW front panels. East Kent's 7021 (PJJ 21S) is seen in Folkestone bus station in 1980. (AS)

The only VR to enter the Black Prince of Morley fleet was this bizarrely painted Willowbrook-bodied example. Black Prince always were a 'fun' operator and the 'one bus on top of another' scheme applied to DGR 874S proves the point. It is pleasing to see the amount of detail that has gone into the design, with even the Bristol VR badge replicated on the upper portion. Seen in Morley town centre, it was new in 1978 as Northern General 3374 and joined the Black Prince fleet in 1990. Sadly, it lasted less than a year and was sold for scrap in early 1991. (RS)

Seen parked at the back of Chepstow bus station is National Welsh XR1952 (OSR 207R), a 1977 Alexander-bodied VRT/LL3. The Alexander body, coupled with the Scottish registration number, give a hint that the bus wasn't new to the Land of My Fathers. It was one of five of the long and low variant of the VR acquired in 1981 from Tayside. Arriving as dual-doored vehicles, the centre exit was removed before entering service. It lasted long enough to make it into Stagecoach ownership before being withdrawn in 1998. (RS)

We're topless again with a wonderfully nostalgic picture of one of Western National's convertible ECW-bodied VRT/SL3s. New in 1978 and delivered to the Devon General division (hence the red and white livery), 943 (VDV 143S) was one of the eleven strong Warship class and was named Ark Royal. In the 1980s, a handful were transferred to Cornwall and 943 is seen in Falmouth with a Bedford of Grenville of Camborne chasing it up Killigrew Street. (RS)

I'm not altogether sure how, but apparently the delightful looking additions round the headlights of Lincoln City Transport's East Lancs-bodied VR 32 (EFE 32T) were to stop the mirrors from getting dirty. Maybe the dirt took one look at those horrors and decided to stay away? New in 1979, it would survive long enough to pass to Lincolnshire Road Car when the Lincoln fleet was acquired in 1994. (RS)

I've included this picture to show the difference between the low- and full-height VRs, but by sheer coincidence it includes another vehicle that ended up with Lincolnshire Road Car – Yorkshire Traction's 905 (XAK 905T). Looking the same as the NBC era, the lack of logo on either bus, the Frontrunner logos either side of the destination blind on East Midland's DWF 194V and lack of any form of uniform for the driver indicate that we are in the early days of privatisation. The location is Hartley Street, Mexborough. (RS)

During the busy summer months we used to press whatever was available to duplicate National Express services from Cornwall. Quite often a Western National Leyland National or VR would appear at Plymouth's Bretonside bus station, such as seen here with 1132 (AFJ 697T) having arrived on the 321 from Porthleven in September 1990. (PG)

Staying with the Cornish theme, a company I have had a long association with is Roselyn of Par, who incidentally purchased the majority of the ex-UK AERE AEC Regents as well as three of the VRs discussed on page 71. Another VR operated was former East Midland and Stagecoach South Coast AET 186T, which acquired Cornish registration number BCV 91T and is seen surrounded by its contemporaries at Par depot in 1999. (PG)

Eastern Counties were one of the biggest VR operators, and took the last examples delivered to the NBC. They also acquired several second-hand examples from a variety of sources and making the move from the Midlands to the flatlands was 140 (BRF 691T), which was new to Potteries in 1978. Seen here in Norwich Surrey Street bus station carrying Counties' post-privatisation livery but after the company had become part of FirstBus (as it was then), it was transferred in 1992 and lasted a further six years before succumbing to the cutter's torch in 1998. (MH)

Staying in Norfolk, Great Yarmouth Transport were one of the few municipal operators to order ECW-bodied VRs, though the bodies being built in nearby Lowestoft might have been an influencing factor. Here PVG 24W skirts the roundabout in front of Britannia Pier wearing its attractive traditional colour scheme. The four W-registered VRs were the first Yarmouth buses to be fitted with ticket machines as before 1981, Yarmouth still used conductors! Like most of the fleet, it passed to Eastern Counties when Yarmouth became part of FirstBus in 1996. (MH)

January 1982 saw the last VRs to be registered arrive at Northampton Transport, a batch of six fitted with East Lancs bodies. When Northampton too became part of FirstBus, half of them passed to – yep you've guessed it – Eastern Counties. 336 (ABD 72X) is seen loading in Castle Meadow, Norwich. (PG)

The highest numbered VR chassis and so believed to be the last one to be built was UVT 49X, an ECW-bodied example delivered in 1981 to that fascinating independent, Stevensons of Spath. It is seen here in 1987 on a private hire to Wembley Stadium – I'm not sure who would be the most pleased to get there, the driver or the passengers! It ended its days in preservation but was stolen in 2013 and is presumed scrapped. (AS)

A feast of VRs in Selby bus station with two carrying the short-lived West Riding Selby fleetname. Facing the camera is 898 (PWR 448W), a Series 3 VRT new in 1981, while the other two are Series 2 models. Behind 898 is 805 (HHL 736L), while on the left of the picture with its back to the camera is 800 (GHL 191L), West Riding's first VR. Withdrawn in 1995, 898 was exported to New York, where it joined the Gray Line fleet as an open-topper. (RS)

And to finish the VR chapter, we're back down in Cornwall. Sandwiched between four VRs is one of the ex-London Transport DMS class Daimler Fleetlines that arrived in the early 1980s to replace ageing Leyland Atlanteans. It's noticeable how the additional height (and maybe shape) of the DMS has rendered it more prone to being bashed by trees. Despite none of the buses displaying any destinations to confirm it, this is the back of the old Newquay depot. Interesting that the two VOD-registered VRs on the left, despite being only two numbers apart, have managed to acquire different styles of number plates. (MH)

The Bristol LH

The final single-deck model to be built at Bristol was the LH (Lightweight chassis, Horizontal engine), which was first introduced in 1967 and immediately available on the open market – indeed some of the first customers for the LH were from the independent sector. The LH came in three lengths, the standard LH at 30 feet long, the LHS (LH Short) at 26 feet, and the LHL (LH Long) at 36 feet. The LH was available with a choice of engines, either the Leyland O.400 (later replaced by the Leyland O.401) or the Perkins H6.354, usually mated to a Turner-Clark synchromesh five-speed with overdrive on top gear. However the Self-Changing Gears semi-automatic box was available as an option.

There was no intention of the LH range being aimed squarely at bus operation, and while the majority of standard length LHs were built as buses, the little LHS had an almost fifty-fifty split between bus and coach and all the LHLs built for PSV use were bodied as coaches. The non-PSV chassis were eleven LHLs and three LHs built between 1973 and 1982 and bodied as pantechnicons for Wilson's of Guiseley, makers of the famous Silver Cross pram, and CUT 730K, an LH built as a race-car transporter for Wheatcroft of Leicester. Nearly every mainstream UK bodybuilder built on the LH platform; however, only one received a body by Weymann. This was MBO 1F, the first LHS built. This bus was delivered to Western Welsh in 1968, three years after the Weymann factory closed, the body originally having been fitted onto an Albion Nimbus delivered to Western Welsh in 1961. The body was extended to allow its wheelbase to match the chassis and it received a Lodekka-style grille to provide cooling for the radiator. It later passed to Thornes of Bubwith and is currently preserved.

The LH remained in production until the end of chassis manufacture at Bristol; indeed, the only 'Y' suffix Bristols were three Plaxton Supreme V-bodied LHSs, and altogether nearly 2,000 were built: 1,505 LH, 174 LHL and 308 LHS.

The prototype LHS, chassis LHX/3, was delivered to Western Welsh in 1968 and was registered MBO 1F. It was fitted with a unique Weymann dual-purpose body that was originally fitted to a 1961 Albion Nimbus-registered WKG 27. The compact little bus is seen in 1974 parked in Bridgend bus station and happily still survives in preservation with Thornes Coaches. (AS)

The first three production LHLs built were all fitted with Plaxton Panorama bodies and delivered to Golden Miller of Feltham, with TMT 765F the last of the trio. Seen here after being relegated to a seat store with Meredith's of Malpas in Cheshire, it refused to give up turning a wheel and subsequently passed to a driving school in Bristol before being scrapped in 1989. (MH)

In 1968, Ivory Coaches of Tetbury and associated fleet Byngs of Portsmouth each received one of the first LHs delivered, both with Plaxton Panorama bodies. PBU 857F is seen at Southern National's Weymouth coach station when brand new. Both Ivory and Byngs were under the ownership of Lancashire Motor Traders, hence the Oldham registration. (AS)

Marshall of Cambridge built two body styles for the LH, one of which was this neat little design that only appeared on the LHS. In the eight years the design was available, only nineteen were built. The first four were delivered to Southern Vectis in 1969 and 834 (NDL 770G) is seen in Newport bus station in 1970. Note the British Road Services Austin 'Noddy van' in the background (AS)

Only a handful of LHs received Plaxton Derwent bodies, including RDE 660G, one of a pair of dual-purpose seated LH6Ls delivered to Silcox of Pembroke Dock in 1968. By 1970, both had received rather garish brightwork around the front panel, which does little to enhance its appearance. (RS)

I'll bet the driver of East Midland's LH6L 0529 (UNN 529G) was a popular chap – less than two months old when this picture was taken in Beetwell Street, Chesterfield, it had already suffered accident damage to its lower offside skirt. It was one of only ten LHs fitted with a Willowbrook body, all of which were delivered to East Midlands in June 1969. (AS)

In May 1969, the associated Mansfield District/Midland General fleets received ten forty-five-seat ECW-bodied LH6Ls, four going to the Mansfield fleet and six to Midland General. One of the former was 107 (BNU 669G), seen in Mansfield shortly after delivery. (AS)

Coity Motors began operating a bus service between the village of Coity and Bridgend in 1923. During the sixty-two years the company was in operation, it only purchased one Bristol – Plaxton Derwent-bodied ATG 459H, the only LHL to receive a bus body. In 1983 disaster struck Coity when the garage was destroyed by fire, with the LHL being one of the casualties. (AS)

The only companies to receive dual-door ECW-bodied LHs were Wilts & Dorset and Hants & Dorset, both companies being under a common management at the time. The additional door saw a loss of four seats, and according to anecdotal reports the centre doors were very rarely used. Hants & Dorset's LH6L 3027 (REL 744H) was new in 1970 and is seen a year later in Fareham bus station. (AS)

As far as I am aware, the only other dual-doored LHs were the twenty bodied by Northern Counties for Lancashire United in late 1969 and early 1970. 333/332 (UTD 296/5H) are seen enjoying the north-west England sunshine while on an excursion to Blackpool in 1975. (AS)

The narrow axle track of the LH always made them seem a little 'top heavy' when fitted with coach bodies, especially a purposeful looking body like the Duple Commander. South Midland's 37 (YBL 926H) is one such beast and was an LH6L new in 1970. Seen with coaches from Shropshire on its left and South Wales on its right, it is parked in Oban on an extended tour in 1971. (AS)

In 1970, United bought five Plaxton Panorama Elite-bodied LH6Ls specifically for use on extended tour work, hence the single-track destination display. Delivered in United's attractive olive green and cream livery, they were later repainted into National white and found themselves operating National Travel services. 1085 (BHN 985H) is seen far from home approaching Cheltenham coach station in 1975. (AS)

Eastern Counties purchased the LH demonstrator and went on to buy a further sixty-six examples, the majority of which were fitted with Perkins engines. ECW-bodied LH916 (YPW 916J) was new in 1971 and was caught on camera at the Old Cattle Market bus station in Ipswich in 1971. (AS)

Another operator to purchase one of the three demonstrators was Golden Miller of Feltham. However, by the time it arrived with Golden Miller, the company had already purchased nine Plaxton-bodied LHs and would go on to buy a further ten plus one Duple Dominant. They ran all three lengths of LH and seen in Princes Park, Eastbourne is Plaxton Panorama Elite-bodied LHL6L GME 981J. (AS)

I was wondering how to get my obligatory Yelloway picture into a book on Bristols when MH came to my rescue with this little cracker. Seen on the coach park in Weston-super-Mare (which also doubles as their parking area) are two of Baker's finest. Back when this photo was taken, Baker's had a very varied fleet, and a visit to Weston always included a wander round their vehicles. On the left is a bit of a rarity, CDK 409C, a Harrington Legionnaire-bodied Bedford VAL that was new to Yelloway, and on the right is a Plaxton Panorama Elite-bodied LHL6L JHS 460K, new to Southern of Barrhead and one of only three LHLs delivered new to a Scottish operator. (MH)

Just like fellow London operator Golden Miller, the Ewer Group also operated all three lengths of LH, and just like Golden Miller they were all Plaxton-bodied apart from one Duple. Ewer's LHs were allocated to the Grey Green and Orange Luxury fleets and one of the latter was Plaxton Panorama Elite-bodied JRK 626K, a 1972 LH6L seen in Eastbourne when brand new. (AS)

Known affectionately as the vodkas, Western National's Marshall-bodied LHSs were split between the Devon General and Western National fleets. Bought as replacements for a batch of Albion Nimbuses (or should that be Nimbi?), the DG examples arrived early enough in 1972 to receive DG's traditional red and cream livery before succumbing to NBC poppy red and included 92 (VOD 92K), seen in Exeter bus station when brand new. (AS)

When Bristol Omnibus needed a small bus to operate the Windmill Hill Community Bus service they borrowed VOD 93K, sister ship to the bus above. Finding the LHS suited the needs of the route, two ex-London Country examples were purchased in 1980, and seen in its special Windmill Hill livery is 1501 (RPH 108L), formerly London Country BL8. As a lad I used to ride this route quite often, and with two regular drivers and friendly regular passengers it was a lovely way to spend a day. (RS)

The last 'flat front' LHs were six ordered by Wigan Corporation and were due to be given 'M' prefix registrations. However, the 1974 Local Government reorganisation saw the Wigan fleet engulfed into the mighty Greater Manchester PTE and the LHs didn't arrive until later that year, thus receiving 'N' plates. 1322 (BNE 765N) is seen in Wigan depot, where the LHs spent their entire GMPTE service lives. (RS)

I mentioned earlier that Marshall built two body styles for the LH, and here's the second one. Ten of these rather graceful bodies were built on standard LH chassis and delivered to Western National painted in Royal Blue livery. They were built to 7-foot 6-inch width for use on tour work around Dartmoor and Exmoor and were the last vehicles to be delivered in Royal Blue livery. Within a year they had been painted into National white livery as seen on 1323 (NTT 323M, departing Cheltenham coach station in 1975. (AS)

Only three LHs received Duple Dominant bus bodies and all were delivered to Welsh operators. Davies of Pencader had one and the other two were delivered to Silcox of Pembroke Dock, who seemed to have a thing about rare Bristols. LDE 166P is seen leaving the yard at Pembroke Dock. (RS)

Even rarer was HJF 233N, one of only two Duple Dominant coach bodied LH6Ls. New to the Leicester County Convalescent Homes Society, it was kept in a purpose-built garage at the convalescent home in Sheringham. For some reason, for the last few years of its time in Norfolk it stayed locked in the garage and the company I worked for did all the work it should have done. In 1992 it passed to Aero Tours and is seen arriving at Spalding for the Tulip Festival in May 1995. (RS)

I may be wrong, but I think the six LH6Ls delivered to Wallace Arnold in 1975 were the only Bristols ever to be operated. Split evenly between the Wallace Arnold Devon and Embankment of Plymouth Fleets, all had Plaxton Panorama Elite III coachwork. HWU 83N was photographed in Keynsham, near Bristol. On withdrawal by Wallace Arnold, all remained in the south-west, four passing to Cornwall County Council and two, including this one, to Deeble of Upton Cross. They were intended to be fitted with 7-foot 6-inch wide bodies but production problems at Plaxton saw them end up with full width bodies. (RS)

The majority of bus bodied LHs new to small independent operators went to Welsh companies, with Daniel Jones of Carmarthen topping the table with five – four ECW and a lone Plaxton Derwent-bodied specimen. JCY 478N, an LH6L new in 1975, is seen passing Carmarthen bus station on Jones' local service. It passed with the rest of the Jones fleet to Davies of Pencader in 1978. (RS)

The last two Duple Dominant-bodied LHLs were delivered to Wimbledon-based Wilde (Wimco), a company who have traded as Mitcham Belle for nearly a hundred years. JGP 237N, the first of the pair, is seen in 1975 parked in Eastbourne's Princes Park coach park after completing its inaugural journey. (AS)

Another vehicle that was almost brand new when caught on camera was London Transport's BS3 (GHV 503N), a 1975 Bristol LHS6L with twenty-six-seat ECW body. Seen at Swiss Cottage on a C11 working from Highgate Archway, it was sadly involved in an accident when less than three years old and was withdrawn in 1978. (AS)

Greater Manchester PTE's coaching unit was made up of four subsidiaries, each with the same livery style but in differing colours. The largest unit was Charterplan, based at Charles Street in Stockport. The smallest coaches in the unit were three Duple Dominant-bodied LHS6ls, the first of which was 92 (JND 992N), new in 1975 and seen in United Counties' Luton depot in 1978. (AS)

No, your eyes aren't playing tricks on you, this really is a very narrow, very short coach. Despite being more or less in the shadow of the Leyland factory, a requirement for some small vehicles saw Preston Bus turn to Bristol. The order was for three Duple Dominant Express-bodied LHSs but with 7-foot 6-inch wide bodies, creating this rather bizarre look. 342 (PHG 242P) is seen at Deepdale Road depot. (AS)

The old established Cornish company Harvey of Mousehole (pronounced Mowzel), in partnership with Western National, operated the Penzance–Newlyn service that travelled through the narrow streets of Mousehole and so required small vehicles. Harvey's were one of two independent operators to order the Marshall body on the LHS and seen in Penzance bus station is PCV 178R. (RS)

Apart from some Bristol Ks in the 1940s, the only Bristol chassis delivered to London Transport were the LHS/LHs, which arrived between 1975 and 1977. Intended mainly to replace ageing RF class AEC Regals, they were 7-feet 6-inches wide due to restrictions at certain locations (at Kingston garage, one of the last RF strongholds, the restriction was the width of the inspection pits). Most were withdrawn by the mid-1980s, and like several of the class BL64 (OJD 64R) ended its days with Guernseybus. (AS)

During 1983/4, South Yorkshire PTE introduced a group of 'Nipper' branded routes to service locations inaccessible to full-size buses. Several LHS6Ls were purchased from London Country including TPJ 60/5S, formerly BN60 and BN65 respectively. Sheffield services were branded as 'The City Nipper' with buses carrying a red-based livery. Rotherham services were just branded as 'The Nipper' and used a brown-based livery, with one of each seen here. (RS)

Western National also used 7-foot 6-inch wide LHs but fitted with coach bodies, firstly Plaxton Panorama Elites and latterly Plaxton Supremes. Initially bought to operate tours across Dartmoor and Exmoor, in later years they were spread across the Western National group and Supreme-bodied 3306 (AFJ 726T) is seen exiting London VCS. (AS)

We've seen the angular Marshall body for the LHS and the curvy one for the LH – well here's a combination of the two. GVO 159V was one of only two built, both for Gash of Newark. They were the only independent operator apart from Harvey's to order Marshall-bodied LHSs.

In 1981 British Airways purchased five Plaxton Supreme IV-bodied LHS6Ls for staff transfers and internal work at Heathrow Airport. By 1991, RLN 227W, the first of the five, had travelled north to Manchester Airport and is seen travelling through Manchester Piccadilly. (RS)

I make no excuse for including the other 50 per cent of Harvey's LHS fleet, as KRL 444W was the only ever Bristol fitted with Wadham Stringer bodywork. Harvey's was taken over by Grenville Motors in 1986 with Grenville themselves taken over by Western National in 1988, thus making the Newlyn service 100 per cent Western National's. Seen prior to receiving the Blue Bus name given to the former Harvey's operation, KRL is seen travelling down Market Jew Street in Penzance. (RS)

The last bus bodied LH built was Rossendale Transport's 51 (SND 551X), a 7-foot 6-inch LHS6L with East Lancs body. One of two delivered in 1982, it is seen in Rawtenstall bus station in its first days of service. Allegedly sold for preservation in 1998, it was never collected by its new owner and so passed to Silver Star of Caernarfon, where it was scrapped after being stripped for spares. (AS)